Your New Beginning

*A Hope-Filled Guide to Living Out Your Purpose
and Reaching Your Promised Land*

Frank Garguilo

To all who believe in new beginnings.

Trilogy Christian Publishers

A Wholly Owned Subsidiary of Trinity Broadcasting Network

2442 Michelle Drive

Tustin, CA 92780

For information, address Trilogy Christian Publishing

Rights Department, 2442 Michelle Drive, Tustin, Ca 92780.

Trilogy Christian Publishing/ TBN and colophon are trademarks of Trinity Broadcasting Network.

For information about special discounts for bulk purchases, please contact Trilogy Christian Publishing.

10 9 8 7 6 5 4 3 2 1

Library of Congress Cataloging-in-Publication Data is available.

ISBN 979-8-89041-153-2

ISBN 979-8-89041-154-9 (ebook)

TABLE OF CONTENTS

Acknowledgments

I want to thank my family for always loving and supporting me, especially Mom for instilling in me a belief in new beginnings and Dad for passing on the drive to pursue my dreams. Thank you, Grandma for anchoring our family and helping us see good in the world. To Victor, for your vital role in designing my dream farm. To Barb, Kevin, Michele, and Charlie for your steadfast lifelong friendship, and to Marcia for believing in me from the beginning of my journey.

Special thanks go to my mentor Mary Morrissey, for giving me a true understanding of how life-transformational principles can not only change lives, but change the world. To MaryAnn Crockford, thank you for so beautifully orchestrating my vision and ideas into a masterpiece. This book would not be what it is today without you.

Finally, to Jesus Christ my Lord and Savior, thank you for the gift of salvation and making a New Beginning possible for all of us!

PREFACE

Henry David Thoreau was the caretaker on Ralph Waldo Emerson's Concord, Massachusetts estate. Emerson had read in the Bible that Jesus said, "they will do even greater works than these."[1] He was so intrigued by this idea that he invited several people to his home to ask important questions about the nature of the universe. Out of these meetings grew the American Transcendentalist movement, which would include great writers such as Thoreau, Louisa May Alcott and Nathaniel Hawthorne, the great Romantic author. These meetings came to be known as the Concord Conversations. Thoreau wanted to go beyond these conversations and conduct his own experiment regarding the laws of the universe there on Emerson's Walden Pond. He lived deliberately for two years, two months, and two days and concluded:

> If one advances confidently in the direction of his dreams, and endeavors to live the life which he has imagined, he will meet with a success unexpected in common hours. He will put some things behind, will pass an invisible boundary; new, universal, and more liberal laws will begin to establish themselves around and within him; or the old laws be expanded, and interpreted in his favor in a more liberal sense, and he will live with the license of a higher order of beings.[2]

Most of the great motivational speakers and writers base their teaching on Thoreau's philosophy and Napoleon Hill's book, *Think and Grow Rich*. I have written this book to clearly show that these principles are successful because they originate in the

Word of God. It's my intention to demystify these truths so that anyone can understand and apply them to his or her own life, using as a metaphor the Israelites' journey out of slavery in Egypt to their Promised Land. Through their journey, you will see these principles active in the mindsets of Moses, Joshua, and Caleb as they lead their fellow descendants of Abraham beyond faulty generational thinking to the freedom that was their birthright as God's chosen people. As you read, you will see yourself in this story because you, too, are chosen and destined for greater things than you ever imagined! But first I will share my own story, my own journey, starting a few decades ago with my own new beginning.

CHAPTER 1
My Story: A Message of Hope

"All I have seen teaches me to trust the Creator for all I have not seen."[3]

—Ralph Waldo Emerson

I grew up in Central New York in the 70s, hanging around horse barns and shows. All the great local horsemen talked about the grandeur of Kentucky, the home of so many great champion horses. In 1973, Triple Crown-winning thoroughbred Secretariat was named by Time Magazine "Super Horse" of all time.[4] In 1976 the great American Saddlebred show horse, Will Shriver, won the five-gaited World Championship. I was in awe of these great horses and wanted to visit Kentucky and be a horseman myself, so I spent my teenage years working with that dream in mind. In the spring of 1983, after my second year of college, I decided to sign up for a nine-week summer horseshoeing course in Mt. Eden, Kentucky that was owned and taught by Don Canfield, who was actually Will Shriver's farrier. Pulling into the town of Mt. Eden was like taking a Sunday drive back in time. Friendly, slower-paced, and endowed with the most charming southern accent, the people I encountered there brought a delightful kind of culture shock. Local old-timers sat outside the general store in rocking chairs, sharing news and rehashing their favorite stories. At the back, the cook served up burgers and daily specials at a single round kitchen table. Sitting at that table, I became family and was invited to add my own story to the local lore. Watching Little League teams compete on an old baseball diamond was the highlight of the week, as was attending Sunday service at the local Baptist church pastored by a fire-and-brimstone preacher whose message of repentance and salvation surprisingly spoke to my Italian Catholic soul. The farrier college was located in an old elementary school that had been converted into dorms and a single forge area where students learned to shape metal into horseshoes. As part of the farrier program, my fellow students and I would travel daily to horse barns throughout the Bluegrass region, where we practiced trimming the hooves of thoroughbred and saddlebred broodmares. One day we stopped in Versailles, which is the premiere location for saddlebreds, to eat lunch at a local diner. As we walked in, there was an oil painting of Sultan's Santana, who had recently become the first saddlebred horse to sell for a million dollars. I said to myself that I would love to own a horse of his caliber someday.

As time went on, I fell in love with the Kentucky horse culture and its equine estates with rail wood fencing and ornate iron entrance gates. The barns were impressive with their traditional stalls with all brass finishes, and massive cupolas with copper roofs. I felt at home in these surroundings and instinctively knew that one day I would live there and own a Kentucky-style barn, where I would train my own horse and show it at the Lexington Junior League horse show and the State Fair World Championship. I finished out the program and became a certified farrier in August of '83 and headed back to New York to start a horseshoeing business. Recalling what I'd learned from a life-transformational course I took in high school based on Norman Vincent Peale's *The Power of Positive Thinking*, I set about creating a vision board and a list of goals to become a successful farrier. My list, which I faithfully read upon rising and going to bed every day, included converting a milk truck into a mobile blacksmithing service. As faith would have it, within the next week, I was driving down the road and came across an old milk truck for sale, in good condition, for $600.00! I purchased it and converted it into the horseshoeing van I'd envisioned, complete with a gas-fired forge and a built-in bed in the front. Granted, it could only go 45 miles per hour, but it was mine, and within two years, I was operating a successful farrier business.

Another dream on my list was to return to Kentucky to attend the World Championship Horse Show that featured the world's best American Saddlebreds. I had purchased a plane ticket and was all set to attend the 1985 Kentucky State Fair and watch the grand horse show. The power of positive thinking seemed to be working for me, and I was excited that in three days I would be fulfilling yet another lifelong dream. Then two days before I was to leave, a horse I was shoeing lost its footing, slamming me into the concrete pad and falling directly on top of me. I sustained a spiral fracture of my tibia, and arrived at the hospital where they set my leg in a cast and sent me home. The next morning, I woke up spitting up blood and unable to breathe. My dad rushed me to the hospital, where I told the nurses that I felt feverish, only to be told that my temperature was actually normal.

While waiting for the results of x-rays of my lungs, back in my room I told my mom, "Something is seriously wrong with me. I feel like my spirit wants to leave my body."

I remember that it was exactly 4:00 that afternoon when I closed my eyes and realized that the power of positive thinking wasn't going to be enough to heal me. But just as clearly, from the depths of my soul, I believed in that moment that God could. I fell asleep to this revelation and awoke twenty minutes later to the sensation of a warm breeze blowing over my body and what I can only describe as a jolt of power hitting me in the middle of my chest. I knew something supernatural had just happened to me, and I was going to be okay, but I didn't fully understand it as I fell back asleep.

I awoke again later to my whole entire family outside my room, and the doctor's diagnosis of a pulmonary embolism—a blood clot caused by a fragment of bone marrow from the spiral fracture—circulating in my bloodstream and coagulating in my lungs. The doctors informed us that if the embolism went from my lungs to my heart, at twenty-two years old, I could suffer a heart attack. Still, somehow, I knew I would be all right and told my grandmother as much. The family matriarch and a woman of faith, she held my hand and said, "Yes, you are, Frank."

My healing process took well over six months, during which I joined a Catholic Bible study with a friend. Six of us met weekly, and it was led by a woman who spoke of Jesus as though he was her best friend, and I was intrigued that she was so full of life and joy.

One night, a few weeks into the study, I cried out to Him for help with my own internal struggle to find peace. That night as I fell asleep, I again experienced that sensation of a warm breeze blowing over my body that I had felt in the hospital months earlier. But this time I experienced fear, and thought, *Why is this happening to me?* At that moment, I felt an urgency to open up my Bible to find the answers I needed. It occurred to me that growing up I had gone to church every Sunday and attended Catholic religion classes, but I had never personally read the Bible.

I started with the Gospel of John, and after reading the full life story of Jesus there was a change in my spirit. To my amazement, I could fully understand the Good News of the Gospel, and at that moment God, became real to me! I accepted the gift of forgiveness through the death of His Son and repented from my sins. I was redeemed and became a new creation through His resurrection power. I was so grateful for this New Beginning and could not have predicted all the doors He would open as I entrusted my life to Him.

In the spring of 1986, I started working for US Airways at the Hancock International Airport in Syracuse, New York. This job brought me the ability to travel all over the world, and I was able to build lifelong friendships with co-workers and people I met. When US Airways restructured in 1991, I had a chance to transfer to the Tompkins Regional Airport in Ithaca, New York.

There was also a supervisor position open at the Lexington Bluegrass Airport, and I thought, *This is my chance to live my dream and own a horse farm in Kentucky!* I interviewed for the position, but it went to a more experienced candidate, and I went to work at the airport in Ithaca. I was disappointed, and at times I questioned the likelihood of achieving my Kentucky dream.

One day, while driving among the hills around Ithaca looking for a place to live, I saw out of the corner of my eye a pair of Morgan horses with their heads hanging out of their Dutch stall doors. I pulled into the driveway and introduced myself to the Crispell family. We became good friends, and they invited me to live with them on their Abundant Life Farm. Over the next two years that I lived with them, I observed what a truly authentic relationship with God looked like, in which He loved and provided for them in all their humanity. This was an entirely new concept for me, that He loves us unconditionally and desires to bless us. I will share later in this book what I observed of this family's faith that would become life-transforming for me.

After living there for two years, I ventured out to build my own farm, having decided that my current circumstances dictated that I would not be moving to Kentucky anytime soon. I had it in mind to build a traditional Kentucky style horse barn right where I was. While traveling the local countryside, I came across a piece of land with spectacular views and rolling hills, so I turned in to the driveway and knocked on the door of the little farmhouse. A gentleman in his eighties answered the door. I introduced myself, explaining that I had been struck by the neighboring farm's beautiful views as I was driving by, and I asked if he knew the owner. He said, "My name is Elmer," and then he introduced me to his wife, Minnie. "We own the land." I asked if it was for sale, and he said, "Yes it is, and I want $50,000.00 for the 32 acres and large turn-of-the-century bank barn." He then added, "You can get it appraised if you'd like, but I am not taking a penny less and I will hold the mortgage with $7,000.00 down."

Without hesitation I said, "It's a deal," and I shook his hand. I put all my savings into that down payment and became the owner of thirty-two acres of land and a well-built bank barn with hand-hewn beams.

The following spring, I built a small turnout shed for my two horses and moved into the large barn with a refrigerator and portable toilet as my only amenities and started to convert the barn into living quarters. I had no building experience, but I had the drive to achieve my dream, and I was willing to learn the rest. Within a couple of years, I had built a beautiful home with eighteen-foot ceilings and four horse stalls on the first floor. Life was great, and I was very happy to be living my dream of owning my horse farm when circumstances would again interrupt my plans. I received the news that my brother's kidneys were failing, and he asked me if I would donate one of my kidneys to him. Of course, I said yes.

After the surgery, I experienced a dramatic change in my mental health and began to experience constant, overwhelming fear for no reason. I was only thirty-two years old, but a deep fear of growing old began to consume me, along with dark thoughts about my self-worth and I lost touch with reality. Then depression and anxiety led me to thoughts of suicide, and one morning I decided to swallow both bottles of the antidepressant and anxiety medications I had been taking. I experienced an eerie calm as I laid down on my bed, and fell asleep expecting to die. A friend checked in on me, and when he couldn't revive me, I was rushed by ambulance to the hospital where I had my stomach pumped.

When I woke up in the hospital bed, I said out loud, "I wish I had died." I found myself in the psychiatric ward, where I felt only shame, regret and humiliation that I had done this to myself even though everything I had ever wanted seemed to be happening. Not only had I veered off the path, but I had fallen into a deep, dark hole. I didn't know how I was going to make it out of such a terrible situation, but the inner voice I now recognize as the

Holy Spirit spoke through the fog promising that God's grace would show me the way. The climb out of that hole took about ten years, but with His help I eventually overcame my pervasive anxiety and depression. Most everyone goes through dark periods in life, but these periods can be powerful times of learning and transformation. Looking back, I can see that my near tragedy gave me an inner strength and compassion for myself and others going through difficult times. I want to assure you that through the power and grace of God, there is always hope, no matter how dark things might seem.

Fast-forwarding, the fall of 2008 brought the mortgage crisis and the bursting of the real estate bubble. That spring I had decided to become a real estate agent, thinking this would be my career, but when the market collapsed I had to take on two other jobs to make ends meet, and I did this for three years. This situation grew tiresome and I became discouraged and discontented with the circumstances of my life.

One night in the winter of 2012, after feeding my horses, I turned on the TV and my favorite movie, Secretariat, was on. In one scene, Penny Chenery's brother wants to sell Secretariat because he's starting to show real promise as a great racehorse, and they could sell him for enough money to pay off the debts of the family horse farm. But Penny refuses, saying, "I will not live the rest of my life in regret. This is not about going back. This is about life being ahead of you and you run at it! Because you never know how far you can run unless you run."[5]

At that moment, Penny's words spoke to my soul and forever altered my mindset. I made the decision that I was going to move to Kentucky and this time, nothing would stop me from getting there. Over the next six months, I made arrangements with my friends Betsey and Kevin, the only two people I knew who lived in Kentucky, and I put my farm up for sale. Within a week it sold and I quit my job, packed my truck, and loaded my horse Redford into the trailer and headed south. We arrived in

Paris that weekend, and surprising things began to happen that showed me God was orchestrating events in my life. That same weekend, the Secretariat Festival happened to be taking place there in Paris, and I was able to meet Penny Chenery and her groom and jockey! And days later, I was hired as a sales and design expert for Lucas Equine Equipment, the manufacturer of some of the world's finest horse stalls and barn equipment.

Doors continued to open, and soon I was able to purchase five acres of land there in Paris. I broke ground for my Kentucky-style barn that would include a cupola with a copper roof—my lifelong dream was finally materializing. I was even living in the same township where Secretariat had stood at stud at the famous Claiborne Farm! Betsey and Kevin were in awe of how things were falling into place for me and said, "Things just seem to happen for you, Frank."

But looking back now, my success was really never about me being luckier or more gifted than anyone else. Rather, it was a combination of the decisions I had made over time, and my refusal to entertain doubts as I pursued my dream. Within a couple of years, I finished construction on my barn and was living the life I'd always wanted. Yet, I longed for something more. Something connected to my life's purpose was still missing. To help me identify what that was, I had begun to read books written by some of the most influential life-transformation experts, especially Napoleon Hill and Jack Canfield. In Canfield's groundbreaking book *The Success Principles*, he asks the question, "What were you put on this Earth to do?"[6] This reminded me that in high school, I had wanted to be a motivational speaker.

A couple years after reading the book and growing in my understanding of life-transformational principles, I decided to quit my job and become a certified life coach. Excited to truly live out my purpose, I flew to California to study under Mary Morrissey at the Brave Thinking Institute. In one of her masterful training classes, she described Jesus as "the most evocative human being that ever lived."[7]

She spoke of His unique ability to draw out people's true divine nature. This was also when I learned about Henry David Thoreau's famous experiment, and could look back over my life and see clearly that the principles he wrote about were indeed true. I had been met "with a success unexpected in common hours,"[8] at times in spite of myself.

That entire week became an "Aha!" moment for me that cemented my life's purpose: As a Christ-centered life coach, I wanted to serve others by using my gift of encouragement and what I'd learned by applying these proven success principles in my own life. I had a strong desire to help others to look beyond their own circumstances and conditions, so they could grow in their faith and start imagining the abundant life God intended for them as His highest form of creation. And that is exactly why I have written this book. Each chapter focuses on a time-tested and -proven success principle which works *because* it was first established by the Creator.

CHAPTER 2
The Beginning: Your Purpose and Vision

"It has been said that the two most important days of a man's life are the day he was born and the day on which he discovers why he was born."[9]

—Ernest T. Campbell

When we read in Genesis about the creation of the world, we get our first glimpse into the mind of the Creator. Just as there is an order of authority or hierarchy to God—Father, Son, and Holy Spirit—there is an order in the process of creation:

Let us make mankind in our image, in our likeness, so that they may rule over the fish in the sea and the birds in the sky, over the livestock and all the wild animals, and over all the creatures that move along the ground.

Genesis 1:26

God imagined and spoke the universe into existence, with mankind as his highest form of creation. This position gives us the authority to co-create with Him a life that is free, joyful, and of immense benefit to others! While all creation adapts to its environment, we are the only creatures that actually *create our own*. You are made in His image so you are creative by nature and influence your environment with the thoughts, words, and beliefs you act upon. Until you grasp this important concept, you will lack direction like the Israelites did, because so many of them did not fully understand what it meant to be purposely designed with a chosen destiny. But their leaders Moses, Joshua and Caleb did understand this, so they were able to actively lay hold of their identities and life purposes.

> Before I formed you in the womb I knew you, and before you were born I set you apart
>
> Jeremiah 1:5

The Creator has set you apart, too, and to navigate the journey toward your destiny, you need to know your purpose. The single most important question you can ask is, *What did He create and set me apart to do with my life?* After that, *What gives my life a sense of direction and meaning and makes me feel fully alive?*

Moses, Joshua, and Caleb knew that their purpose was to lead their people safely through the wilderness and across the Jordan River into the Promised Land. You have been created for a great purpose, too, and connecting it with something you are passionate about is the key to discovering just what that purpose is. With this exciting truth in mind, let's now work on discovering your purpose. Take out a notebook and pen and keep them handy, because going forward you'll be completing some brief written exercises designed specifically to help you with this and other crucial steps in your journey.

Action step: Identifying Your Purpose

Most of us struggle at some point to find our purpose. It's okay if you aren't quite sure what yours is yet. It can feel like an intimidating proposition at first, so I encourage you to take some time and ask God to help you in this process.

Here is an exercise that can help you start identifying your life's purpose: Write down two or three gifts you possess that can be of benefit to you and others. Examples might include the ability to encourage, the gift of compassion, a great sense of humor, leadership skills, or any ability or strength that applies to you. Also write down several ways you have used these gifts to serve others. Now combine these two ideas—your gifts and how they have served others—into a single statement. If you're not sure how to do this, you can use my own purpose statement as a template: "My purpose is to use my gifts of encouragement and enthusiasm to help others live the life God intended for them."

CONGRATULATIONS! Through this exercise, you have taken a courageous first step toward fulfilling your dreams: Identifying your purpose, the thing you know you were born to do!

"Purpose: how you use your experiences, talents, and passions to better the lives of those around you."[10]

—Lindsay Peterson

The Power of Vision

"You can't hit a target you cannot see, and you cannot see a target you do not have."[11]

—Zig Ziglar

The next step is one all life-transformational teachers place great importance on, and that is to create a clear vision that serves your purpose. Moses, Joshua, and Caleb never lost sight of their target destination, the Promised Land. They each had a strong vision that always kept them moving toward it. God also places great importance on vision, as we can read in Proverbs 29:18: "Where there is no vision, the people perish."[12] As co-creators with Him, we also operate at our best when we have a clear vision that serves our purpose. To begin creating your vision, it's important to seek wisdom from the Holy Spirit and get in touch with what brings you life and a sense of joy. Is there something you love doing so much that even thinking about it makes you feel more expansive and alive?

Action Step: The Desires of Your Heart

In your notebook, write down something that makes you feel expansive and alive. Search your heart. Answering this question can direct you to the life you are longing for! Next, write down what you're discontented with in your life, that makes you feel contracted or confined. This is an important step, because getting in touch with these emotions can help you formulate a clear vision of the life you desire.

> Delight yourself in the Lord, and He will give you the
> desires of your heart.
>
> Psalms 37:4 ESV

A strong vision can change the world and even alter the course of history! Moses was called to lead the Israelites out of captivity and set their feet on the path to the Promised Land. Joshua and Caleb, military leaders, were tasked with protecting their people during a perilous journey in which they were chased by armies and confronted with a race of giants. So, what caused these men to ignore warnings of sure defeat when they looked at their circumstances?

In addition to having a purpose founded on the promises of God, they had something else: They had a clear vision to fulfill their destiny of leading the Israelites and forming a new nation, and nothing was going to stop them. They believed in their purpose so completely that they never fell victim to the same patterns of thinking that would cause the first generation to remain stuck and die in the wilderness, and never know the joy of reaching the Promised Land.

Let's talk now about another man whose vision changed the course of history, the Reverend Martin Luther King, Jr. He was purposefully descriptive and specific about what he wanted his legacy to be for the world. Here are some excerpts from his famous "I Have a Dream" speech given in Washington, D.C. on August 28th, 1963:

> Let us not wallow in the valley of despair. I say to you today,
> my friends, that in spite of the difficulties and frustrations of
> the moment, I still have a dream. It is a dream deeply rooted
> in the American dream.

I have a dream that one day this nation will rise up and live out the true meaning of its creed: We hold these truths to be self-evident, that all men are created equal.

...I have a dream that my four children will one day live in a nation where they will not be judged by the color of their skin but by the content of their character.

I have a dream today.

...I have a dream that one day every valley shall be exalted, every hill and mountain shall be made low, the rough places will be made plain, and the crooked places will be made straight; and the glory of the Lord shall be revealed, and all flesh shall see it together.[13]

Like King, you will now begin creating a clear, strong vision statement that serves your life's purpose. When designing your Promised Land vision, ask yourself what you would love your life to look like forty months from now. Why forty months? I've chosen this number because it aligns with the Israelites' forty-year journey out of slavery into freedom. This number of months will also be necessary to create a truly life-changing vision, one that shifts your focus away from your present circumstances and the doubts that can prevent progress. When laying out your vision, you will need to get in touch with your longing and discontent. These are important emotions to pay attention to, because they will guide you to a life of joy and contentment. It's important not to limit your imagination as you go through this process. Allow yourself to dream big and get in touch with what makes you feel expansive and alive.

"All things are possible if a person believes."[14] (Mark 9:23)

Action Step: Blueprinting Your Vision

Before you start writing your vision seek God for guidance and ask Him to give you clarity!

Once again, take out your notebook and pen. Write your forty-month vision statement in the present tense, as though you're already living in your Promised Land. This might seem like an overwhelming task, so for now just do the best you can. Focus on writing a statement that includes your desired occupation, relationships, finances, and your overall health and well-being. Express gratitude and personalize it in any way that makes it meaningful for you. This exercise should be inspiring and fun! Below are some examples of how to start writing your vision statement by first breaking it up into these four key areas of your life. Use these examples to guide you as you focus on creating the life you would love to live:

"God, I am so happy and grateful to have reached my Promised Land."

"I am so happy and grateful today for this satisfying occupation that prospers me and benefits others." Describe this satisfying occupation in detail. What does your daily routine look like? What do you love most about your work? How does it bring good to you and others?

"I am so happy and grateful today that I have these fulfilling, healthy relationships in my life." Describe these relationships in detail and how they enrich your life. Include anyone that's important to you.

"I am so happy and grateful today that I am financially secure, which gives me the freedom to do the things I love doing." Describe some of the things that financial freedom is allowing you to do for yourself and others that you couldn't do before.

"I am so happy and grateful today that I am living this life of health and well-being." Describe in detail what a life of health and well-being means to you, and what steps you are taking to achieve it.

GREAT JOB! Now that you have discovered your purpose and are beginning to blueprint your vision, there's one more step to take. You need to establish a strong vision of what your ideal intimate relationship with your Creator looks like forty months from now. Write these things down in your notebook, because you are going to start a new habit right now. Every morning and every night going forward, you're going to read your purpose statement and vision out loud. It's also important that you start expressing gratitude each day and imagine your new life *as if it already exists!*

Important facts to know: When writing your vision down with a pen and paper, you are stimulating a collection of cells in the base of your brain known as the reticular activating system. The (RAS) acts like the ignition system of the brain, that awakens an individual from sleep to a state of heightened awareness. Activating this part of your brain will highly increase your chances of reaching your dreams!